STUDENT UNIT

# A2 Law
# UNIT 2573

## OCR

Module 2573: Criminal Law Special Study

Chris Turner & Leon Riley

A2 Law

Philip Allan Updates
Market Place
Deddington
Oxfordshire
OX15 0SE

tel: 01869 338652
fax: 01869 337590
e-mail: sales@philipallan.co.uk
www.philipallan.co.uk

© Philip Allan Updates 2006

ISBN-13: 978-1-84489-021-7
ISBN-10: 1-84489-021-X

All rights reserved; no part of this publication may be reproduced, stored in a retrieval system, or transmitted, in any form or by any means, electronic, mechanical, photocopying, recording or otherwise without either the prior written permission of Philip Allan Updates or a licence permitting restricted copying in the United Kingdom issued by the Copyright Licensing Agency Ltd, 90 Tottenham Court Road, London W1T 4LP.

This guide has been written specifically to support students preparing for the OCR A2 Law Unit 2573 examination. The content has been neither approved nor endorsed by OCR and remains the sole responsibility of the authors.

Printed by Raithby, Lawrence & Co. Ltd, Leicester

**Environmental information**
The paper on which this title is printed is sourced from managed, sustainable forests.

# Contents

## Introduction
About this guide .................................................................................................. 4
How to use this guide ......................................................................................... 5
Learning strategies ............................................................................................. 5
Revision planning ............................................................................................... 6
Assessment objectives ....................................................................................... 7
The examination ................................................................................................ 8
Using the source materials ................................................................................ 9

## Content Guidance
About this section ............................................................................................. 12
**Statutory interpretation**
    The reasons for interpretation ..................................................................... 13
    The two approaches ..................................................................................... 14
    The three rules ............................................................................................. 14
    The language rules ....................................................................................... 16
    Presumptions ................................................................................................ 16
    Intrinsic and extrinsic aids ............................................................................ 17
    Summary of Source 1 .................................................................................... 18
**Robbery**
    The offence of robbery ................................................................................. 19
    The meaning of force ................................................................................... 19
    The requirement of force being immediately before or at the time of stealing .. 20
    Summary of sources ..................................................................................... 20
**Burglary**
    The offences of burglary .............................................................................. 23
    The definition of building ............................................................................. 24
    The meaning of entry ................................................................................... 24
    The requirement of a trespass ..................................................................... 25
    The ulterior offences ..................................................................................... 25
    Summary of sources ..................................................................................... 26

## Questions and Answers
About this section ............................................................................................. 32
**Question 1** Statutory interpretation ............................................................... 33
**Question 2** Robbery ....................................................................................... 40
**Question 3** Burglary (I) ................................................................................... 45
**Question 4** Burglary (II) .................................................................................. 52

# Introduction

## About this guide

This study guide is written for students following the OCR A2 Law course and covers the specification content for **Unit 2573: Criminal Law Special Study**. The selection of the topics in this module is designed to give students a sound understanding of the two substantive themes of robbery and burglary within the context of the overarching theme of the role of judges, precedent, the application of statutory materials and the development of the law, with particular emphasis on statutory interpretation. This unit is synoptic and therefore, unlike the other two Criminal Law option papers, it requires you to show an understanding of the connections between your studies of the English legal system and of the criminal law.

There are three sections to this guide:
- **Introduction** — this section gives advice on how to use the guide, some learning strategies, hints on planning revision and a reminder of the assessment criteria and how to achieve them. It also gives an explanation of what the exam paper is about and the skills required to complete it successfully.
- **Content guidance** — this section sets out the specification content for Unit 2573, and the key knowledge for successful completion of the exam. It is broken down into sections in the same way as the specification and provides a structure for your learning. Where cases or statutes are referred to, you will need to study these in more detail for a fuller understanding. Unlike the other option papers, you will need to be aware of the materials contained in the special study booklet. This booklet contains useful information on statutory interpretation, robbery and burglary, derived from primary materials such as adapted extracts from cases and from sections of the **Theft Act 1968**, as well as from secondary sources such as leading criminal law texts. These materials will be available to you during the exam itself and throughout your course, so you should learn how to make use of them as references. However, the materials are not definitive in themselves and you should be prepared to bring to the exam your full knowledge of the necessary subject content.
- **Questions and answers** — this section provides sample answers to typical examination questions on each topic area. The four types of question covered are:
  – question 1, based on Source 1, a critical piece of writing on aspects of statutory interpretation
  – question 2, a digest of a case contained in the materials
  – question 3, a piece of critical writing on either robbery or burglary
  – question 4, problem solving based on three short, factual scenarios
  Each question is followed by an A-, a C- and an E-grade answer. Examiner comments show how marks are awarded or why they are withheld.

## How to use this guide

The Content Guidance section covers all the elements of the Unit 2573 specification, breaking down each topic into manageable sections for initial study and later revision. It is not intended to be a comprehensive and detailed set of notes for the unit — the material needs to be supplemented by further reading from textbooks and by your own class notes.

You should also have a good working knowledge of the materials contained in the special study booklet, which you will be able to use in the exam as a source of reference and on which the questions are based. The source materials are not repeated in this book, as these will be supplied by your teacher. However, a summary of the key points made in each separate source is contained in the Content Guidance section.

At the end of each topic section, you may find it useful to compile a summary of the factual material under appropriate headings. Ideally, you should incorporate additional material drawn from a number of sources, for example classroom teaching, textbooks, quality newspapers, law journals and legal websites.

When you have finished compiling your notes, you can tackle the questions in the third section of the guide. Read the questions carefully and answer them fully. You should then read the sample A-grade answers and compare these with your own in order to identify where you could have gained more marks and achieved a higher grade. Compare your answers with the C-, and E-grade answers in order to get an indication of how well you are performing. The examiner comments will help you to gain an understanding of what can limit your marks and how to attain the higher grades.

## Learning strategies

A2 is very different from AS and more is required of you in the examinations. While a good knowledge of the various topics is still important at A2, you will need a greater depth of understanding than you had at AS and you will need to learn many more cases. For this reason, you must keep a clear and accurate set of notes. Another significant difference at A2 is that you are expected to have more highly developed critical ability, meaning that you will need to show that you can discuss the law critically (essays in questions 1 and 3, and the case digest in question 2) and apply the law effectively to factual situations (problems in question 4).

You should employ an effective learning strategy as follows:
- Try to take notes in class in a logical and methodical way; do not just write down everything that the teacher says.
- Make sure that you read your notes again after each lesson so that the information stays fresh in your mind.

- If you do not understand something in your notes, either read about it in your textbook or ask your teacher. Make sure that you correct your notes so that you understand them.
- Do the specific reading that your teacher suggests and also try to read around the subject in order to build up greater knowledge and understanding. If you have spaces in your class notes, you can add additional information from your reading. If not, you should rewrite your notes to incorporate it.
- Be sure that you have a sound working knowledge of the individual sources in the special study booklet.
- Build up a good understanding of the principles of law that come from the individual cases and try to remember the case names by testing yourself frequently. In this unit, the individual sections and subsections of the **Theft Act 1968** are also important.
- Use a legal dictionary so that you are familiar with all the appropriate legal terminology.

## Revision planning

Revision is not the same as learning. All the learning strategies mentioned above should have been covered during the course, and you should have a complete and accurate set of notes when you begin your revision. If you have to learn the material from scratch before the exam, then you are putting extra pressure on yourself.

There are various rules for good revision practice that you should follow:
- Organise your material before you begin. You will be revising more than one subject and there will be several topics in each subject. It will help your revision process if you have separate folders for each subject. By using folder dividers you can turn straight to the topic you wish to revise.
- Organise your time effectively. Thirty minutes preparing a timetable at the start of your revision will save you a lot of time later on. Divide the time you have available by the topic areas and identify how many times you can revise them and then create a chart.
- Use effective revision aids to help compress the subject matter or put it into visual form to make the process simpler and less time consuming. Examples are key fact charts, mind maps, flowcharts and diagrams. Use the materials supplied in the special study booklet.
- Make revision cards on all the leading cases.
- Ask your friends and family to test you on important knowledge.
- Practise past papers. The more familiar you are with the style of questions that you can expect in the exam, the more confident you will be in answering them. Tackling problem questions in particular will help to improve your understanding, since the law makes more sense when it is applied to factual situations.
- Do your revision in short bursts. The longer you sit looking at your notes in one session, the more likely you are to get bored and not take anything in. Take plenty of breaks between sessions.

## Assessment objectives

Assessment objectives (AOs) are the measures against which examiners test your knowledge, understanding and legal skills. They are common to AS and A2 units and are intended to assess a candidate's ability to:

- AO1 — recall, select and develop knowledge and understanding of legal principles accurately by means of example and citation, i.e. your ability to remember the appropriate law, including cases or statute where appropriate.
- AO2 — analyse legal material, issues and situations, and evaluate and apply the appropriate legal rules and principles, i.e. your ability to engage in a balanced discussion, offering points of criticism in essays, and to apply legal rules to factual situations in problem-style questions.
- AO3 — present a logical and coherent argument, communicating relevant material in a clear and effective manner, using appropriate legal terminology, i.e. your ability to give legal information and to discuss or apply it clearly, as well as to spell, punctuate and use grammar accurately.

Remember that in OCR A2 exams, there are five levels of assessment, while for AS there are only four. This means that you have to show more knowledge and better analysis or application skills in order to reach the highest mark level.

For AO1, this means that as well as demonstrating that you have well-developed knowledge, as you did for AS, you must also show this to be wide ranging.

For AO2 you must show a high level of analysis or application, and not just analyse the more obvious points or apply the obvious law, as you would have done at AS.

When you sit AS examinations, you have only completed 1 year of the A-level course. After 2 years, you should have gained more knowledge and have developed better skills. Do not assume that just because you got a good grade at AS, you will automatically do so at A2.

There is also an extra level for AO3, so your communication skills should have improved, and for the highest level you will be expected to write with few, if any, errors of spelling, punctuation and grammar.

The other critical point to remember in the Unit 2573 examination is that the weightings for the assessment objectives are very different from those in the option papers. In the Special Study, only 30% of the marks are available for AO1. This is because the area of study is narrow and also because of the amount of support you are given in the materials booklet. AO2 is worth 60% of the marks and the remaining 10% is for AO3. So, while your knowledge is still important, it is how you apply it that counts in this exam. You must be able to appreciate the significance of statutory interpretation in developing the criminal law and the significance of individual cases in their application of the statutory provisions. You also need to be able to consider the areas of robbery and burglary in a critical way in the context of the development of the law, and to apply legal principles accurately and efficiently.

## The examination

The Unit 2573 examination comprises four questions and you have to answer **all** of them.

### Question 1
This is an essay-style question and, for the duration of the current theme, it is on statutory interpretation. You are expected to show a critical understanding of statutory interpretation in the context of the development of the law. You do not have to specifically use cases from the criminal law to illustrate your understanding. Any cases you may have studied during your AS year that help to illustrate the points you are making are acceptable in the exam. Question 1 is specifically looking for a discussion, so you must be able to identify the critical purpose of the question asked, to engage in a balanced discussion looking at both sides of an argument, and finally to reach conclusions arising from that discussion. You must also be able to illustrate your critical comments with case law. Question 1 is worth either 25 or 30 marks.

### Question 2
This is a digest of one of the cases that appear in the special study booklet. For the duration of the current theme this is on either robbery or burglary. There are only 13 of these cases, so you should be able to learn about each of them comfortably. In any case, much of the necessary detail is given in the booklet. In the exam you must be able to show that you have a full understanding of the significance of the case to the development of the law on robbery or burglary and its application of the specific statutory principle(s) involved. This may mean citing other cases in your answer, since 'development' demands that you either know where the law developed from or where it developed to. Question 2 is worth 15 marks.

### Question 3
This is an essay-style question based on a quote from one of the sources. For the duration of the current theme it is on a narrow aspect of either robbery or burglary in the context of the development of the law. You are expected to engage in a critical discussion, providing a balanced argument and reasoned conclusion, together with supporting law, all in the context of the development of the law. Question 3 is worth either 25 or 30 marks.

### Question 4
This is a problem question comprising three parts. For the duration of the current theme it involves legal problem solving on either robbery or burglary or a mixture of both. You will be provided with three small factual scenarios and you will have to identify the aspects of the law that could be used to resolve the various issues that arise. In criminal law, this means that you will need to identify offences that may arise from the facts. Question 4 is worth 30 marks, 10 marks for each of the three separate scenarios.

Planning is an important part of achieving high marks in any examination. For the essay-style questions (questions 1 and 3), although these are narrowly focused and

only allow half the time usually available for Section A questions on the option papers, you should still remember the importance of structuring your answer, which should include:
- an introduction identifying what the question is asking
- a balanced discussion using cases, sections of Acts and legal principles in support of your answer
- a reasoned conclusion deriving from your discussion

For the case digest (question 2), you need to refer back to the source for the important information contained in it. Remember to include, in brief form:
- the important facts and, if appropriate, other cases for AO1
- the critical issues in terms of the place of the case in the development of the law in question for AO2

You should get used to looking at the sources immediately before and after the one in question, since they are likely to contain other information that is relevant to the development of the law.

For the problems in question 4, remember again the importance of structuring your answer. You should:
- identify for each individual aspect of the problem the key facts on which resolution of the problem is based
- define the appropriate law accurately
- apply the law sensibly to the facts
- reach sound conclusions based on your application of the law

Remember also to:
- read each question thoroughly, so that you understand it fully and can give an accurate answer
- refer back to the appropriate source for further information
- plan your answer briefly at the start of the exam, to ensure you only use relevant information
- always use law (cases or statutes) in support of your arguments for essays or in your application for problem questions
- avoid excessive use of the facts of cases — it is the principle that is important
- make sure that your time management is good — you will have shorter time scales than for the option papers

## Using the source materials

The source materials are there to help you. They are available to you during the year to support you in your learning. You also have them in the exam itself, so you can refer to them for additional support and use them in your answers.

Spending a few moments before answering the question highlighting all the useful information in the source will save you time. More importantly, you will not miss anything in the source that you can use in your answer. It may be a good idea to differentiate between factual information and those aspects of the source that can gain you AO2 marks.

When writing your answer, do not merely copy the information from the source. Use aspects of the information to support your own discussions. For instance, you may think that something a judge or an author has said is relevant to your answer; if you could not say it better in your own words, or you are short of time, then refer to the specific lines of the source so that the examiner can see you are sensibly selecting and citing valid information. This is an important legal skill in itself and can be rewarded. General references to the source as a whole are unlikely to gain credit.

# Content Guidance

The areas covered in this guide correspond to the three sections into which Unit 2573 is divided as follows:

## Statutory interpretation

- The reasons for interpretation
- The two approaches
- The three rules
- The language rules
- Presumptions
- Intrinsic and extrinsic aids
- Summary of Source 1

## Robbery

- The offence of robbery
- The meaning of force
- The requirement of force being before or at the time of stealing
- Summary of sources

## Burglary

- The offences of burglary
- The definition of building
- The meaning of entry
- The requirement of a trespass
- The ulterior offences
- Summary of sources

# Statutory interpretation

## The reasons for interpretation

Statutory interpretation is the process where judges are called on to give meaning to words in an Act of Parliament that are in dispute. Often there is no need for interpretation where the meaning of the words and the intention of Parliament when passing the Act are absolutely clear. However, there are several situations where interpretation may be necessary. These include:

- **Bad drafting** — the person drafting the Act uses the wrong word. In *Fisher* v *Bell* (1960) the words 'offer for sale' were used where 'invitation to treat' would have been the appropriate phrase in contract law. As a result, Parliament had to pass another Act.
- **Ambiguous words** — where the words have more than one meaning. In *R* v *Allen* (1872), applying the meaning 'being validly married' to the words 'shall marry' would have made the offence of bigamy unworkable. The court applied the words 'going through a marriage ceremony' instead.
- **Technical or legal meaning**. In *Beswick* v *Beswick* (1968) the words 'other property' were held to refer only to land and interests in land, because that is what the Act in question concerned.
- **Social or technological developments** — because many things change over time or could not be contemplated when the legislation was passed. In *Royal College of Nursing* v *DHSS* (1981) the words 'registered medical practitioner' under the **Abortion Act 1967** required interpretation. The words originally only referred to a doctor. However, by the time of the case nurses rather than doctors were carrying out the procedures and the House of Lords accepted that this was legal.
- **Broad terms**. An example of this is *Brock* v *DPP* (1993) where the words 'type of dog' were used, and the problem was whether this referred only to the breed of the dog, or had a wider meaning.

Judges use various rules and aids in interpreting statutes and in all cases they try to find the intention of Parliament when the Act was passed. The problem is that the rules can produce very different results and therefore the process is unpredictable. In order to interpret statutes, judges have at their disposal:

- two approaches
- three rules
- three language rules
- various presumptions
- intrinsic aids and extrinsic aids

# The two approaches

- The **literal approach** is where interpretation relies mainly on the words in question, without necessarily referring to anything else.
- The **purposive approach** is a modern approach, resulting from membership of the EU and is the style of interpretation favoured in Europe. The approach is concerned with discovering and giving effect to the purpose for which the legislation was passed and is not so preoccupied with the words in question. An example is *Royal College of Nursing* v *DHSS* (1981) where, even though the words 'registered medical practitioner' only referred to doctors, the House of Lords accepted that nurses could conduct a major role in abortions because the clear purpose of the **Abortion Act 1967** was to ensure that abortions were carried out under clinical conditions.

# The three rules

## The literal rule

This rule, preferred for most of the nineteenth and twentieth centuries, demands that the words should be given their 'plain, ordinary literal meaning', even though this might lead to a 'manifest absurdity', as stated by Lord Esher in *R* v *City of London Court* (1892).

The problem is that words do not always have plain meanings; they may have several different meanings so that absurdities can occur, as in *Whiteley* v *Chappell* (1868) where an election fraud went unpunished because it was held that a dead man would not be 'entitled to vote'.

Focusing only on the words themselves can lead to illogical results as in *IRC* v *Hinchey* (1960); the judges ignored income tax that had already been paid in their interpretation of the words 'three times the amount owed'. It can also mean that Parliament has to pass another Act to resolve the difficulty, as in *Fisher* v *Bell* (1960).

More importantly it can lead to injustices. A classic example is *London & North Eastern Railway* v *Berriman* (1946) where a widow was denied compensation for the death of her husband. He was killed while oiling points on a railway line, and compensation would only be payable if he had been 'relaying or repairing' the line. The court held that 'relaying or repairing' did not include 'maintenance', taking the words of the **Fatal Accidents Act** for their literal meaning.

In *Magor & St Mellons* v *Newport Corporation* (1950), Lord Denning was critical of the literal rule and suggested that instead, judges should use the mischief rule and 'fill in the gaps' if necessary. He was criticised in the House of Lords when Lord Simonds called this a 'naked usurpation of the legislative function'.

The Law Commission has also been critical of the literal rule. In its 1969 report it argued that 'to place undue emphasis on the literal meaning of words is to assume an unattainable perfection in draftsmanship'.

## The golden rule

The golden rule is, in fact, a subsidiary of the literal rule, so it is only used by judges who prefer to use the literal rule. It is also only used where using the literal rule would lead to an absurdity. Lord Blackburn explained the golden rule in *River Weir Commissioners* v *Adamson* (1877) as 'giving the words their ordinary signification, unless when so applied they produce an absurdity or inconvenience so great as to convince the court that the intention could not have been to use them in their ordinary signification and to justify the court in putting on them some other signification'.

The rule can be used in one of two ways:
- **The narrow approach** — here, if the word in question is ambiguous and using the plain meaning can lead to absurdity, the judge will use another meaning which does not. An example is *R* v *Allen* (1872) where the plain meaning of the words would have prevented any convictions for the offence of bigamy and made the Act unworkable. Another example is *Adler* v *George* (1964) where the words 'in the vicinity of a prohibited place' were held to include 'in' the prohibited place, or again an illogical acquittal would have occurred.
- **The broad approach** — here the word is not ambiguous but giving it the plain meaning would prove unacceptable, so for policy reasons the judges prefer to give it a different meaning. The obvious example is *Re Sigsworth* (1935) where the court held that the word 'issue' did not include a person who had killed his mother and then tried to claim his inheritance.

The problem is that there are no real guidelines for when the rule should be used, which is why Professor Zander calls it an 'unpredictable safety valve'.

## The mischief rule

This is the oldest of all the rules and it comes from *Heydon's Case* (1584), which outlined a four-point procedure:
1 Examine the common law prior to the passing of the Act.
2 Identify the 'mischief' or defect in the previous law.
3 Identify the way in which Parliament proposed to remedy the defect.
4 Give effect to it.

Examples include *Smith* v *Hughes* (1960) where 'public place or street' was held to include a first-floor balcony from which a prostitute was soliciting, in order for the court to secure her conviction. *Corkery* v *Carpenter* (1951) concerned a man being drunk in charge of a bicycle, and is another example where, in recognition of technical changes since the Act was passed, 'carriage' was held to include 'bicycle' in order to protect other road users.

# The language rules

There are three language rules concerned with how words are applied in certain circumstances:

1. ***Noscitur a sociis*** — meaning a word is known by the company it keeps. In *Beswick v Beswick* (1968) the words 'other property' were held to refer only to land or interests in land (referred to as 'real property' by lawyers) because the words came from the **Law of Property Act 1925**, which was only concerned with land.
2. ***Expressio unius est exclusio alterius*** — meaning that the express mention of one thing in a list impliedly excludes other things not included in the list. In *Tempest v Kilner* (1846) a list in a section of an Act included 'goods, wares and merchandise'. As a result, the section was held not to apply to 'stocks and shares', which had not been included in the list and could therefore not have been intended to fall under the Act.
3. ***Ejusdem generis*** — meaning 'of the same type'. The rule applies where there is a list of specific words that are then followed by general words. To fall within the scope of the provision, the general words have to be of the same type as the specific words. In *Powell v Kempton Park Racecourse* (1899), the words used were 'house, office, room or other place used' for betting', so the provision could not apply to the outdoor betting area in question, as all the specific places in the list were indoors.

# Presumptions

Judges often presume certain things to be true unless the contrary can be proved. Examples include:

- Parliament does not intend to change the common law unless it actually says so in the Act.
- In Acts creating criminal offences, *mens rea* (criminal intent) must always be proved unless the Act identifies the offence as one of strict liability not requiring intent (*Sweet* v *Parsley*, 1970).
- The Crown is not liable unless this is allowed for in the statute.
- The jurisdiction of the courts is not removed unless a specific alternative such as a tribunal is created and given jurisdiction by the Act.
- A person cannot be deprived of his/her liberty unless the Act specifically states this.
- A person will not be deprived of his/her property unless the Act states this.
- No retrospective laws are introduced unless Parliament specifically provides for this. The case of *Burmah Oil* v *The Lord Advocate* (1965) concerning the **War Damages Act 1965** is an example.

# Intrinsic and extrinsic aids

Judges also have different aids that they can use to help them in interpreting words in statutes. These can be either:
- **intrinsic (internal) aids** that can be found inside the statute itself
- **extrinsic (external) aids** that are outside the statute

## Intrinsic aids

These are found inside the Act and can be used by a judge following any of the rules, although some judges preferring the literal rule focus on the words even without using such aids. There are several intrinsic aids:
- **The short title** — this is merely the name of the Act, so while it gives a clue as to what the Act concerns, it is probably of only minor assistance in interpretation.
- **The long title** — some statutes have a long title at the front of the Act which explains what the Act is trying to achieve, i.e. a list of objectives, so this can prove quite useful in interpretation.
- **The preamble** — older Acts contained a detailed preamble at the front, specifying what the statute covered and what it intended to achieve.
- **Margin notes** — these are included afterwards by the person drafting the Act and so are not strictly speaking part of it. They sometimes indicate the purpose of a section.
- **Schedules** — these usually come at the end of a section and often include more detailed information. An example is Schedule 2 of the **Unfair Contract Terms Act 1977** which details tests for determining reasonableness.
- **Headings** — some sections have headings that can be a guide when there is ambiguity.
- **Interpretation sections** — these are a major aid to interpretation, often giving the meaning of the technical words used. A good example is sections 2–6 of the **Theft Act 1968**, which explain the terms used in the offence of theft in s.1 of the Act.

## Extrinsic aids

These are found outside the Act and tend to be used more by judges favouring a purposive approach to interpretation. Some of them have proved controversial. Extrinsic aids include:
- **Dictionaries** — even judges using the literal rule are often prepared to use a dictionary to find the plain meaning of a word.
- **Other statutes** — these can be useful where Acts are drafted in similar terms. The **Sex Discrimination Act 1975** and the **Race Relations Act 1976**, for instance, are written in almost identical terms.
- **Royal Commission reports** — these can be useful where the Commission has led to the legislation.
- **Law Commission reports** — the Law Commission often prepares draft bills and researches areas of law with a view to reform. If these precede the legislation they can be a useful aid.

- **Hansard** — this is the official detailed report of the debates on the bill in the House of Commons and the House of Lords, so it is extremely useful in finding Parliament's intention when passing the Act. However, judges formerly condemned its use, as was seen by the rebukes received by Lord Denning in *Davis* v *Johnson* (1978). Now, following *Pepper* v *Hart* (1993), *Hansard* can be used if certain conditions are met.
- **Travaux preparatoires** — these are preparatory notes for treaties and can be used, for instance, when Acts based on EU law need to be interpreted.

# Summary of Source 1

### Extracts adapted from Ward, R. (1998) *Walker & Walker's English Legal System* (8th edn), Butterworths

Key points in Source 1 that may be useful for AO1 include:
- Lines 30–31: an example of judicial law making.
- Lines 38–42: some indication of why statutory interpretation is needed, which could obviously be useful in an introductory paragraph of the answer to question 1.
- Lines 50–51: an example of ambiguity and uncertainty in the words, meaning that statutory interpretation is needed.
- Line 54: a reference to extrinsic aids.
- Line 60: an example of a case where the literal rule was applied but Lord Denning suggested using the mischief rule instead (*Magor & St Mellons* v *Newport Corporation*).

Key points in Source 1 that may be useful for AO2 include:
- Lines 1–2: traditional view that judges should not make the law but merely apply existing principles.
- Lines 2–3: 'few would now deny that judges have a powerful law-making function'.
- Lines 16–17: all law is subject to change either by Parliament or by the courts.
- Lines 17–20: legislation is 'the ultimate source of law' and Parliament 'has the power to make or unmake any law'.
- Lines 20–23: while judges may be 'reluctant to make major changes', when they do, it can be done flexibly and quickly and can save parliamentary time.
- Lines 34–37: some judges see it as part of their role to create new law, while others feel that this should be left exclusively to Parliament.
- Lines 38–40: where the words of an Act are clear, there is no need for statutory interpretation.
- Lines 44–46: the primary task for the court is to give effect to the meaning of the words themselves.
- Lines 55–59: factual situations where the statute does not provide any guidance so that the judges have to involve themselves in a legislative function.
- Lines 61–62: Lord Denning's views that statutory interpretation should be used to 'fill in the gaps' and to make sense of the statute.

- Lines 60–61 and 62–64: Lord Simond's criticism of Lord Denning's views as being a 'naked usurpation of the legislative function', and that it is for Parliament to pass an amending Act.

# Robbery

Robbery is an unusual offence because it is not only a theft offence but also has connections with offences against the person. In essence, robbery is a theft that is achieved through the use of force. It is therefore an aggravated form of theft. As such it is a serious offence and it is triable only on indictment, with a maximum sentence of life imprisonment. It is treated so seriously because of its links with social alarm and protection of the public. There is also a separate crime called 'assault with intent to rob'.

## The offence of robbery

The offence of robbery is found in s.8 of the **Theft Act 1968**, where according to s.8(1): 'A person is guilty of robbery if he steals, and immediately before or at the time of doing so, he uses force on any person or puts or seeks to put any person in fear of being then and there subjected to force.' The further offence of 'assault with intent to rob', the mode of trial and the maximum sentence are found in s.8(2).

Robbery is a theft offence, so all of the elements of theft must be shown to be present, as well as those elements specific to robbery (*Robinson*, 1977). However, the theft, and therefore the robbery, may be complete as soon as the defendant dispossesses the other of the property (*Corcoran v Anderton*, 1980).

The *actus reus* of the robbery is the *actus reus* of theft (appropriation of property belonging to another) with force or the threat of force before or at the time of the theft.

The *mens rea* of robbery is the *mens rea* of theft (dishonesty and the intention to permanently deprive) and the intentional or reckless application of force.

## The meaning of force

The **Theft Act** contains no specific definition of force but the courts have accepted only minimal force to be sufficient for the offence (*Dawson*, 1976). What amounts to force is to be left to the jury to decide, and force applied to property may be sufficient in certain circumstances, e.g. the wrenching away of a bag from the victim in *Clouden* (1987), although the Criminal Law Revision Committee's 8th report expressed doubts as to whether this should amount to robbery. Force directly applied to the person presents no problems (*Hale*, 1978), even when the force is carried out by one person and the theft by another. The force must be used in order to steal. If it is for some other purpose then it may be an assault or a wounding offence, but it cannot be robbery (*Donaghy*, 1981). Force also includes putting a person in fear of force. Force will usually be applied to the victim of the theft, but it need not necessarily be to that person, as long as it used to steal.

# The requirement of force being immediately before or at the time of stealing

A strict, literal interpretation of this provision would have a limiting effect on the offence, so the provision should possibly mean that the force has a direct bearing on the commission of the theft offence. Certainly force after, and unconnected with, the theft will not amount to robbery (*Gregory*, 1983), although it may do so if it is part of the struggle to escape. This depends on 'appropriation' being seen as a continuing act (*Hale*, 1979). Force used to prevent the alarm being raised may be similarly appropriate (*Lockley*, 1995).

# Summary of sources

## Source 2

### Section 8(1) of the Theft Act 1968

Key points found in Source 2 that may be useful include:
- 'A person is guilty of robbery if he steals' — so you need to remember your definition of theft here.
- '...immediately before or at the time of doing so, and in order to do so... .'
- '...he uses force on any person or puts or seeks to put any person in fear of being then and there subjected to force.'

## Source 3

### Extract adapted from the judgement of Lawton LJ in *Dawson* (1976) 64 Cr. App. R. 170

*Dawson* is a robbery case where the meaning of the word 'force' was questioned. A key point in Source 3 that may be useful for AO1 is:
- Lines 15–16: brief reference to the facts, i.e. jostling the victim so that he lost his balance.

Key points in Source 3 that may be useful for AO2 include:
- Lines 1–4: the fact that because of authorities under the previous law there was no force.
- Lines 5–8: the judgement of the court that the purpose of s.8 was to remove former technicalities and to use simpler language that juries could understand.
- Lines 9–13: discussion by the judge that the word 'violence' in the **Larceny Act 1916** had been changed to 'force', so that the former law was not relevant to the case.
- Lines 13–14: statement by the judge that force was chosen as a word that is 'in ordinary use' and which juries could understand.
- Lines 15–19: statement by the judge that it was for a jury to determine what level of force was necessary for a charge of robbery.
- Line 22: the members of the jury should decide this according to their own common sense.

## Source 4

### Extract adapted from the judgement of Eveleigh LJ in *Hale* (1978) 68 Cr. App. R. 415

*Hale* involves a problem over the time at which the force was applied. Key points in Source 4 that may be useful for AO1 include:
- Lines 2–4: the basis of the offence of robbery, using force 'immediately before or at the time of stealing' and 'in order to steal'.
- Lines 2–5: some of the facts of the case (there was some force used after the theft of a jewellery box).
- Lines 6–9: the definition of theft ('...dishonestly appropriates property belonging to another with the intention of permanently depriving the other of it').
- Lines 10–11: the definition of appropriation ('any assumption of the rights of the owner').
- Line 24: the force involved tying the victim up after the jewellery box was seized.
- Lines 27–30: the force involved one defendant putting a hand over the victim's mouth to stop her calling for help.

Key points in Source 4 that may be useful for AO2 include:
- Lines 4–6: the defendant claimed that there could be no robbery because the force was used after the jewellery box was seized and so could not have been 'in order to steal'.
- Lines 12–15: the judge's assertion that it would be 'contrary to common sense' to hold that the appropriation is over as soon as the defendant lays his hands on the property.
- Lines 19–23: the judge's explanation that appropriation is a continuing act.
- Line 29: the judge's conclusion that the jury would be entitled to conclude that the act of tying the victim up was done in order to steal so that the defendant can be found guilty of robbery, having used force in order to steal.

## Source 5
### Extract adapted from the judgement of Watkins J in *Corcoran v Anderton* (1980) 71 Cr. App. R. 104

A key point in Source 5 that may be useful for AO1 is:
- Lines 2–4: brief reference to the facts of the case (the defendant snatching a woman's handbag and causing it to fall to the ground so that she no longer had control of it).

Key points in Source 5 that may be useful for AO2 include:
- Lines 1–6: the statement by the judge that snatching the bag and causing it to fall to the ground out of the control of the victim is an appropriation.
- Lines 6–9: the judge's statement that even under the **Larceny Act 1916** this would amount to a clear theft.
- Lines 9–11: the judge's statement that this amounts to a clear example of robbery.
- Lines 12–14: the question posed for the court whether, due to the fact that the defendant did not have exclusive control of the bag, this could still amount to robbery.
- Lines 15–19: the statement of the judge that there was appropriation, although some interpretations of the word might produce a contrary view.

## Source 6
### Extract adapted from Smith, J.C. (2002) *Smith & Hogan Criminal Law* (10th edn), Butterworths (p. 563)

This textbook extract discusses the level of force sufficient for a charge of robbery and uses the example of *Clouden*.

A key point in Source 6 that may be useful for AO1 is:
- Lines 11–13: the basic facts of *Clouden* (the defendant wrenched a shopping basket from the victim's hands and ran off with it).

Key points in Source 6 that may be useful for AO2 include:
- Lines 1–2: the author's assertion that the slight physical contact needed to pick a pocket would amount to force.
- Lines 2–4: the author's assertion that very little contact is necessary to amount to force for the purposes of robbery, the example used being jostling sufficient to cause the victim to lose balance.
- Lines 5–9: the former law required that the force should be to overpower the victim, not to take the property, and that the Criminal Law Revision Committee (CLRC) would not have regarded the mere snatching of a purse as sufficient force for robbery.
- Lines 13–17: the court in *Clouden* held that this was inconsistent with the words in s.8 'in order to steal' so that it was open to the jury to decide how much force was necessary for a conviction.

# Burglary

Burglary as an offence has its origins in the Middle Ages. It derived from *'burge breche'* which was a form of breaking and entering at night with the intent to commit a felony. In this way, common-law principles of trespass are at the heart of the offence. The original character of the offence meant that it was always treated more seriously than mere theft because of the extra distress caused to the victim. Consequently, the offence of burglary developed very much in line with early common-law property values. The previous range of offences was limited and complex, so these were reformed in the **Theft Act 1968** and are now contained in s.9, although significantly, there are two separate offences. The offence of burglary is triable either way, for obvious reasons.

## The offences of burglary

According to s.9(1), a person is guilty of burglary if:
**(a)** he/she enters any building or part of a building as a trespasser and with intent to commit any such offence as is mentioned in s.9(2); or
**(b)** having entered any building or part of a building as a trespasser, he/she steals or attempts to steal anything in the building or that part of it or inflicts or attempts to inflict on any person therein any grievous bodily harm.

According to s.9(2): 'The offences referred to in subsection (1)(a)...are the offences of stealing anything in the building or part of a building in question, of inflicting on any person therein any grievous bodily harm, and of doing any unlawful damage to the building or anything therein.'

Therefore, s.9 creates two offences: one involving entering the premises with the intent to commit further offences identified in s.9(2) and one where the defendant, having entered as a trespasser, goes on to commit one or more of a more restrictive range of further offences.

The *actus reus* in either case involves an entry amounting to a trespass into a building or part of a building. In addition, in the case of s.9(1)(b), since one or more of the offences of theft, attempted theft, grievous bodily harm and attempted grievous bodily harm must also be committed, the *actus reus* of the offence in question will also have to be shown.

The *mens rea* differs between the two offences:
- In s.9(1)(a) the intention to commit one or more of the offences identified in s.9(2) must be shown.
- In s.9(1)(b) there is no ulterior intent but the necessary *mens rea* for the offence that the defendant carries on to commit is required.

In either case, intention or recklessness as to the trespass must also be shown.

Burglary, like other theft offences, is very much open to interpretation and most of the terminology used has caused difficulty at one time or another.

## The definition of building

The meaning of 'building' is not absolutely defined in the Act but it is partly expanded upon in s.9(4): 'References in subsections (1) and (2) above to a building...shall apply also to an inhabited vehicle or vessel, and shall apply to any such vehicle or vessel at times when the person having a habitation in it is not there as well as at times when he is.'

It has been said that the imperfection of human language makes it not only difficult, but absolutely impossible, to define the word 'building' with any kind of accuracy. In *Stevens v Gourley* (1859), Byles J concluded that a building was a '...structure of considerable size and intended to be permanent or at least to endure for a considerable time'. Nevertheless, the courts continue to have difficulty in determining what the term 'building' includes. Various 'structures' have been the subject of discussion in relation to burglary. Whether or not they are buildings may depend on their general character as well as on the use to which they are put: compare for instance *Norfolk Constabulary v Seekings and Gould* (1986) with *B and S v Leathley* (1979). More problematic, of course, are temporary structures, such as caravans.

The trespass can also be to part of a building (*Walkington*, 1979). Even though the building may have been entered lawfully, it is important to prove that the defendant then moved to a part of the building, which amounts to a trespass (*Laing*, 1995).

## The meaning of entry

An entry is a key requirement of the offence. In s.9(1)(a) the defendant 'enters' with intent to commit specific crimes, and in s.9(1)(b) 'having entered' the defendant goes on to commit prescribed crimes. In either case, there is no offence without an actual entry into the premises.

The obvious question is the extent to which the defendant has entered the building. In other words, does all of his body have to enter or only part of his body? Traditionally, the entry had to be 'effective and substantial' (*Collins*, 1972). More recently, however, the courts have been prepared to accept that there can be an 'effective' entry without the need for it to be 'substantial' (*Brown*, 1985). In certain circumstances it is clear that the entry does not need to be either 'effective' or 'substantial' in order for the offence to be carried out (*Ryan*, 1996). In the latter case, the intention of the defendant was seen to be more important than his ability to carry out the ulterior offence.

## The requirement of a trespass

The previous law focused on a 'breaking and entering', but the **Theft Act** replaced this with the requirement of a trespass. Trespass is a concept that is associated with civil law and, although it is a complex area of law, it generally involves entering without permission, whether intentionally, recklessly or negligently. Therefore, if a person enters with permission he cannot be a trespasser (*Collins*, 1972). However, it may be considered a trespass where a person has permission to enter but acts in a way that is inconsistent with that permission (*Jones and Smith*, 1977).

## The ulterior offences

The ulterior offences are those laid out in s.9(2) of the **Theft Act**: 'The offences referred to in subsection (1)(a)...are the offences of stealing anything in the building or part of a building in question, of inflicting on any person therein any grievous bodily harm, and of doing any unlawful damage to the building or anything therein.'

The ulterior offences are associated with the s.9(1)(a) offence, and the prosecution needs to show that the defendant had the intent to commit one of these offences when he/she entered the building or part of a building as a trespasser. It does not matter that he/she does not go on to commit one of these offences; it is the intention that is important. There are three ulterior offences:
- theft (stealing)
- grievous bodily harm (GBH)
- criminal damage (doing any unlawful damage)

### Theft

The elements of theft are found in the definition in s.1(1) of the **Theft Act 1968**: '...dishonestly appropriates property belonging to another with the intention of permanently depriving the other of it... .'

### Grievous bodily harm (GBH)

Grievous bodily harm can be the offences under either s.18 or s.20 of the **Offences against the Person Act 1861**. The essential elements of GBH under s.18 are identified as: '...unlawfully and maliciously by any means whatsoever...cause(s) any grievous bodily harm to any person with intent to do some grievous bodily harm to some person or with intent to resist or prevent the lawful apprehension or detainer of any person ... .' The essential elements of GBH under s.20 are: '...unlawfully and maliciously...inflict(s) any grievous bodily harm upon any other person, either with or without any weapon or instrument... .'

## Criminal damage

The basic offence is defined in s.1(1): '...without lawful excuse destroys or damages any property belonging to another intending damage or destruction or being reckless as to whether such property would be destroyed or damaged.'

It is important that you have a good working knowledge of the basic elements of these offences so that you can identify the s.9(1)(a) offence accurately. The questions in the exam will not demand that you write extensively on these offences but you will, in any case, need to know them for your Criminal Law 2 (Unit 2572) paper.

These ulterior offences raise other issues. For instance, it may be possible that a conditional intent to steal will be sufficient (*Attorney General's References (Nos 1 and 2 of 1979)*, 1979). Similarly with 'inflicting grievous bodily harm' in s.9(1)(b) it is arguable that no offence needs to be committed (Purchas LJ in *Jenkins*, 1983).

It is also important to remember that, while the intention to steal, or to commit GBH or criminal damage, are all ulterior offences for the purposes of s.9(1)(a), under s.9(1)(b) the linked offences (having entered the building as a trespasser) are only theft and GBH, and criminal damage is not included. This last point is particularly important when you are examining factual scenarios in problem questions and trying to distinguish between the s.9(1)(a) offence and the s.9(1)(b) offence.

# Summary of sources

## Source 7

### Extract from s.9 of the Theft Act 1968

Source 7 contains various subsections of s.9 of the **Theft Act 1968** — s.9(1)(a), s.9(1)(b), s.9(2) and s.9(4).

Key points in Source 7 that may be useful include:
- The definition of the s.9(1)(a) offence: someone enters a building or part of a building as a trespasser with the intention of committing one of the ulterior offences in s.9(2).
- The ulterior offences for s.9(1)(a): theft, GBH or criminal damage.
- The definition of the s.9(1)(b) offence: having entered as a trespasser someone goes on to attempt or to commit either theft or GBH.
- The extended definition of building in s.9(4): this includes any inhabited vehicle or vessel, including when the occupier is not there.

## Source 8

### Extract adapted from the judgement of Edmund Davies LJ in *Collins* (1973) 1 QB 100 CA

*Collins* is a leading case on burglary in which there was a lengthy discussion on the meaning of entry as a trespasser.

Key points in Source 8 that may be useful for AO1 include:
- Lines 1–5: the brief facts from the case (the defendant intended to enter the house and to rape the girl inside and was either on the outside or inside sill when she invited him in).
- Lines 6–10: the key elements of the s.9(1)(a) offence.
- Lines 13–16: the meaning given to trespass in *Archbold* (any intentional, reckless or negligent entry into a building without the consent of the occupier).
- Lines 17–21: the meaning given by Professor Smith (the requirement of *mens rea* by contrast to the civil law definition).
- Lines 22–26: the definition given by Griew that the defendant must knowingly trespass or be reckless.
- Lines 27–31: the support given to Griew's definition by the court in the case.

Key points in Source 8 that may be useful for AO2 include:
- Lines 11–12: the assertion that the meaning of entry as a trespasser had not previously been discussed in the courts.
- Lines 32–37: the court thought the pivotal point of the case was where the defendant was precisely when he was invited in.
- Lines 38–41: the meaning of 'entry' given by the court in the case (that it must be effective and substantial).

## Source 9

### Extract adapted from Jefferson, M. (2003) *Criminal Law*, Pearson Publishing (pp. 429–30)

This textbook extract discusses developments following from *Collins* in the cases of *Brown* and *Ryan*.

Key points in Source 9 that may be useful for AO1 include:
- Lines 4–5: the basic facts of *Brown* (the top half of defendant's body was in a shopfront display while the bottom half of his body was outside the window).
- Lines 5–6: the basic facts of *Ryan* (the defendant's head and right arm were inside the house but his neck was trapped in the window).

Key points in Source 9 that may be useful for AO2 include:
- Line 1: that the judgement in *Brown* widened the meaning given to 'entry' in *Collins*.
- Lines 3–4: that the court identified the fact that the whole of the defendant's body does not have to be in the building for the entry to be effective.
- Lines 6–7: the Court of Appeal in *Ryan* applied the principle in *Brown*.
- Lines 8–10: the defendant in *Ryan* was unable to do anything effective.
- Lines 11–13: the decision of the court that 'effective' does not have to mean 'effective to commit the ulterior offence' and the comparison used with an entry with the intent to rape when the occupant is not in the building.
- Lines 14–15: the fact that the court felt that effective was to do with the entry, not the ulterior offence.
- Lines 17–19: the restating of this principle.

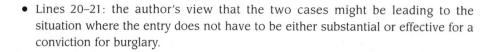

- Lines 20–21: the author's view that the two cases might be leading to the situation where the entry does not have to be either substantial or effective for a conviction for burglary.

## Source 10

**Extract adapted from Molan, M., Bloy, D. and Lanser, D. (eds) (2003) *Modern Criminal Law* (5th edn) Cavendish Publishing (pp. 297–98)**

This is a textbook extract on the meaning of 'building', using various cases to illustrate what has and what has not been accepted as a building for the purposes of burglary.

Key points in Source 10 that may be useful for AO1 include:
- Lines 2–5: the definition given in *Stevens* v *Gourley* (structure of considerable size and intended to be permanent or long lasting).
- Lines 5–12: the facts of *Norfolk Constabulary* v *Seekings and Gould* (attempted entry of two articulated lorries, which were not buildings for the purposes of burglary; even though they were used as temporary storerooms with lighting from an electricity cable, they were still standing on their wheels and their character had not really changed).
- Lines 12–13: the name of another case distinguished in the last case, *B and S* v *Leathley*.
- Lines 19–25: the facts of *Laing* (the appeal was upheld as although the defendant was found in a stockroom after the shop had closed, it had not been suggested that he became a trespasser when moving from one part of the store to another).

Key points in Source 10 that may be useful for AO2 include:
- Lines 1 and 2: s.9(4) gives only limited guidance on the meaning of building and there is therefore no complete definition in the Act.
- Lines 14–16: under the literal rule, 'building' can include smaller units such as flats.

## Source 11

**Extract adapted from the judgement of Lane LJ in *Walkington* (1979) 1 WLR 1169**

*Walkington* is the leading case on the meaning of entry to 'part of a building' as a trespasser.

A key point in Source 11 that may be useful for AO1 is:
- Lines 1–5: the basic facts of the case (the defendant was in a department store and went into an unattended till area not open to the public; he looked into the open till and slammed it shut when he found it was empty and was convicted of burglary under s.9(1)(a)).

Key points in Source 11 that may be useful for AO2 include:
- Lines 10–11: the view of the court that it did not matter that there was nothing to steal.

- Lines 11–15: the fact that it was sufficient that the defendant intended to steal when he entered that part of the building as a trespasser so that conditional intent is sufficient.

## Source 12
### Extract adapted from Clarkson, C. M.V. and Keating, H. M. *Criminal Law Text and Materials* (4th edn), Sweet & Maxwell (p. 834)

This textbook extract discusses the contrast between the civil law and criminal law definitions of trespass and also the principle from *Jones and Smith* on the meaning of trespass.

Key points in Source 12 that may be useful for AO1 include:
- Line 2: the civil law definition of trespass, 'enters without the consent of the person in possession'.
- Lines 9–13: the facts of *Jones and Smith* (son entered his father's house with the intent of stealing television sets so had exceeded the terms of consent to enter and was a trespasser).

Key points in Source 12 that may be useful for AO2 include:
- Line 36: the contrast with criminal law where *mens rea* is required, the defendant either knowing that consent was absent or being reckless as to that fact.
- Lines 7–8: the definition might include legitimate visitors when they go beyond the terms of the consent to their entry.

# Questions & Answers

This section of the guide provides you with examples of all four question types that you will encounter in the Unit 2573 examination. Question 1 is marked either out of 30 or 25 (in the question here it is marked out of 30), question 2 is marked out of 15, question 3 is either marked out of 30 or 25 (in the question here it is marked out of 25), and question 4 is marked out of 30, with 10 marks available for each of the three scenarios. Remember that for this paper it is important that you evaluate or apply the law effectively, since there are only 30 marks available overall for AO1, while there are 60 marks available for AO2. AO3 is worth 10 marks overall.

A-, C- and E-grade answers are provided for each question. The A-grade answers should give you a clear idea of the approach and structure required. They are comprehensive in the knowledge demonstrated and show high-level evaluation or application skills. These answers are usually able to make the best use of the assistance in the source materials. The C-grade answers illustrate some of the problems that result in students achieving lower marks. These answers tend to be quite knowledgeable but do not have the same levels of sophistication in the other skills. E-grade answers are often sketchy with some knowledge shown but not a full appreciation of all the necessary knowledge. They usually ignore the help given in the sources in the special study booklet, which often results in the law or the facts being wrongly stated.

After the answers to each question there is a section identifying the information that can be found in the source materials that you could make use of in the exam.

## Examiner's comments

Each answer is accompanied by examiner's comments, preceded by the icon *e*. These indicate where credit has been given, recognising the candidate's use of the examinable skills, as explained in the introduction. In the C-grade and E-grade answers, the examiner indicates possible improvements that could be made to achieve a higher grade.

Question 1 answers, as well as requiring good AO1 skills of recall of knowledge, also require good essay-writing skills for AO2 and high levels of evaluation and analysis. You will find some useful evaluative material and some key information in Source 1 of the special study booklet.

Question 2 answers require brief selective knowledge for AO1 but should concentrate mainly on AO2 skills, which means that you must show a good understanding of the significance of the case to the development of the particular area of law.

Question 3 answers require the same demonstration of skills as for question 1, except that in this case in-depth discussion is required since the focus is narrow, and needs good concentration on the overarching theme of the development of law.

Question 4 answers require high-level legal problem-solving skills and good application of appropriate law.

# Question 1

# Statutory interpretation

Discuss the extent to which both the literal and purposive approaches to statutory interpretation focus primarily on the words in an Act in order to find out the intention of Parliament.

(30 marks)

■ ■ ■

## A-grade answer

Where the words in an Act of Parliament are clear, there is no problem in applying them. However, there are several problems that can arise when judges are called on to interpret words in an Act to find the intention of Parliament. Because of the nature of the English language, some words are prone to ambiguity and can have more than one meaning. It is therefore difficult for Parliament, as well as for parliamentary draftsmen, to be clear and concise when drafting statutes, as to what Parliament actually intended. The literal approach and the purposive approach are means adopted by the judges to overcome this problem.

Lord Reid in *Shaw* v *DPP* stated that 'where Parliament fears to tread, the judges should not go rushing in'. He was therefore a devoted follower of the literal rule, as he believed that it was not up to the courts to set moral standards. Furthermore, in *Lim Poh Choo* v *Camden Health Authority*, the trial judge also stated that, given the surgical atmosphere of the courtroom, it was not an adequate place to make law.

When using the literal rule, judges do primarily get meaning from the words, as they are supposed to give the words in the Act their plain, ordinary, everyday meaning. However, using the words in a statute in their ordinary, everyday meaning has given rise to absurdity on many occasions.

In the case of *Berriman* v *London & North Eastern Railway Co*, the claimant's husband had been killed while being involved in maintenance work filling oil boxes on the railway line. It was held, interpreting the words in the Act literally, that compensation would only be due if he had been 'relaying or repairing' the line and therefore the claim was unsuccessful.

In *Cutter* v *Eagle Star Insurance* it was held, using a literal interpretation, that compensation would only be due if a person had been injured in a car on the road and not in a car park and therefore the claimant again was unsuccessful.

In the case of *Whiteley* v *Chappell*, the defendant had impersonated a dead person in order to fraudulently use that person's vote. The statute stated that it was an offence to impersonate 'any person entitled to vote' but the defendant was acquitted as the court held that a dead person would not be entitled to vote, allowing the defendant to get away with an election fraud.

# A2 Law

**question**

Therefore, although the literal approach has its merits and does focus mainly on the words, it can lead to absurdity and not to what was Parliament's intention. Judges who believe that they have only a passive role in the law-making function adopt this approach in order to respect parliamentary sovereignty. They would argue that unelected judges should not be able to make laws in this country. However, it is still true that a large amount of English law derives from the common law, for instance the definition of murder. This realisation is also identified in Source 1 in lines 1–6.

> This is a good use of the source, since lines 1–6 identify that the traditional view of the judicial function is 'not to make law but to decide cases in accordance with existing principles'. It goes on to say that 'few would now deny that judges have a powerful law-making function'. Consequently, this part of the response would gain good AO2 credit. It also identifies an important way in which candidates can save time in the special study exam by citing appropriate lines of a source to illustrate a point that they are making, rather than copying out the extract from the source.

Professor Glanville Williams has stated that he believes that any judge who uses the literal rule of interpretation and, for example, the *Oxford English Dictionary* meaning of words, must be either a 'mischief maker, pedant or idiot'. The modern purposive approach is a far more reliable method of finding the intention of Parliament when passing the Act. This is because, in trying to find the purpose of the Act, it still respects the words used by Parliament, but if this leads to some sort of absurdity or repugnance, the words may be interpreted in order to find the mischief that Parliament was trying to rectify.

This approach led to the result in *Smith* v *Hughes*. The defendants were prostitutes who were soliciting from their rooms, one from an upstairs balcony. The statute stated that it was an offence to solicit in the street, but it was interpreted to include the situation in this case because the judge identified that the purpose of the Act was to prevent people from being harassed by prostitutes and so the defendants were guilty.

The purposive approach can also include the golden rule, which can be used to avoid repugnant situations. In the case of *Re Sigsworth*, the defendant stood to inherit all of his mother's wealth after he had murdered her. It was held that the word 'issue' meant that a person was only entitled to inherit where they had not killed the owner of the property, even though the statute did not imply any such idea.

Judges who follow this approach to interpretation include Lord Denning, who was a keen believer that the courts are much better equipped to make law faster and cheaper than Parliament can. Lines 30–32 of the source indicate this.

> This use of the source is not particularly worthy of credit. Lines 30–32 refer to the *High Trees* case and, although the candidate makes the point about judicial law making, this is not in the context of statutory interpretation.

It is true, therefore, that the intention of Parliament should be established primarily from the words used in the statute. However, there are many other aids that can be used, which may make the meaning clearer. The purposive approach has allowed the use of extrinsic aids such as *Hansard*, the daily record of debate in Parliament, which was approved in *Pepper* v *Hart* subject to certain conditions. There are also the rules of language such as *ejusdem generis* and *noscitur a sociis*, which may be used to help establish the intention of Parliament.

> For a 27-minute essay, this response is quite lengthy and detailed. It has a good balance between its knowledgeable use of case law in illustration of the rules and its relevant comment. There is 'wide ranging knowledge' considering the time restraint, and the literal rule is clearly defined and well illustrated. The candidate successfully uses a mischief rule case and a golden rule case for illustrating the purposive approach. The mischief rule is given a reasonable definition, although not the actual rule in *Heydon's Case*. Using the golden rule as an example of the purposive approach is valid, since the broad approach has been used and the way that the rule works has been clearly explained. The definition of the purposive approach itself is slightly thin, but there is a useful link to the use of extrinsic aids, particularly *Hansard*.
>
> There is a lot of comment. This is not always directed absolutely at the point in the essay title, although there is generally a basic argument and there is some good reference back to judicial or academic comment. The candidate has tried to compare the two approaches as the question required, and has tried to make effective use of the source materials. The AO1 is better than the AO2, and the latter could have been improved with a good conclusion. However, there is still enough material to achieve a solid grade A.

■ ■ ■

## C-grade answer

Traditionally, courts have encountered some problems when trying to give effect to the words in statutes. Sometimes this is because the words used are ambiguous, meaning that they can have more than one meaning.

To help with problems such as this, the courts have developed rules. One of these rules is the literal rule, which is where the courts will look at a dictionary and give the words their ordinary definition. They will do this even if it leads to an illogical or unfair result. The literal rule was used in *Fisher* v *Bell* where the defendant was found to be not guilty of 'offering for sale' a flick-knife, which was a prohibited weapon, because the court held that displaying the goods was actually an 'invitation to treat'. As a result, although the rule does stick to the words used in the statute, it does not always achieve the object or purpose of the statute. Therefore, if the courts were always to use the literal rule then many absurd results could occur. This reveals the difficulty of trying to show what Parliament intended from the words themselves. This is shown in lines 56–57 of the source.

> Lines 56–57 refer to having to 'attribute to Parliament an intention which [it] never had', so this is a valid point and would gain credit, although the candidate could have developed it further.

**question 1**

A2 Law

The purposive approach has developed from the mischief rule and it looks at what the general purpose of the statute is and then applies this to the case. This rule was used in *Royal College of Nursing* v *DHSS*, which involved interpretation of the Abortion Act 1967. Under the Act, only doctors could carry out abortions and only doctors did at that time. But by the time of the case it was increasingly likely that the abortion would involve a procedure that was actually carried out by nurses. The court identified that Parliament had intended the Act to work for controlled and supervised abortions, carried out in proper hospitals, and to stop 'back street' abortions being carried out by unqualified people. Therefore, it is clear to see that Parliament had intended to make hospital-supervised abortions legal. The case highlighted that judges can have difficulty in reaching their judgements and that things like expense and morals should not get in the way.

> This is an attempt to make an AO2 point, but it is not clearly argued and it is hard to see exactly what the candidate means.

Both these rules highlight the fact that words within Parliament's definitions often have more than one meaning and it is often difficult for judges to interpret these. This is the reason in lines 45–47 of the source that it is argued that judges should go through two processes in order to reach a decision that will not produce absurd results.

> Lines 45–47 refer to the difference between interpretation, asking 'what do the words themselves mean' and construction, 'the process whereby uncertainties and ambiguities in a statute are resolved'. The candidate would gain some credit for referring to this part of the source, although it could have been developed further.

However, the literal rule and the purposive approach are not enough on their own, and other rules have to be looked at before a court can offer a ruling.

The other rules include the golden rule. This is where, if there is an ambiguous word, the court has to look for a sensible meaning, for example in the case of *R* v *Allen* where if the literal rule was applied then it would be impossible for the defendant to have committed the offence of bigamy. By using the golden rule it meant the word 'marry' was interpreted as 'to go through a ceremony of marriage'.

> The candidate is mixing the two approaches of the golden rule in the definition given and has not identified that the narrow approach is an extension of the literal rule. As a result, only limited credit could be given for the case example.

The mischief rule involves looking at what Parliament meant or the wrong or 'mischief' it was trying to correct. It was successfully used in *Smith* v *Hughes*, where the defendants were 'soliciting' in the street contrary to the Street Offences Act 1958, as the Act was clearly designed to prevent this.

> The candidate has missed the point of the case here.

As stated in line 54 of the source, other extrinsic aids may be used in order to determine Parliament's intention. These can include a dictionary or *Hansard*.

# OCR Unit 2573

> 🅔 Again, the candidate has managed to write at length and include a good amount of detail for a 27-minute essay. There is a substantial range of well-developed knowledge that would be rewarded for AO1. On the whole, good use has been made of cases, although some are used incorrectly, and some points have not been developed as far as they might have been to secure higher marks. The AO2 is much more limited than the AO1. There is no overall argument and not enough focus on the question set. The answer tends to be narrative and contains little discussion — a hallmark of C-grade answers.

■ ■ ■

## E-grade answer

The role of judges is primarily to apply the law. Within statutory interpretation this can be done in different ways using the literal rule, golden rule, mischief rule and purposive approach. The literal rule and purposive approach are completely opposite ways of interpreting statutes and give different results.

> 🅔 The point in the final sentence about 'opposite ways of interpreting statutes' has the potential to be a very good opening AO2. However, it lacks any kind of development or illustration so could only gain minimal credit.

The literal rule is the way that judges interpret to make sure that no new law is being created. This is done by applying the law word for word. Because of this, judges are only allowed to use intrinsic aids such as short and long titles to decipher the ambiguous words.

> 🅔 A valid point is made in the first sentence but overall the definition is limited. The final sentence is not quite accurate and misses the obvious point that literalist judges also use dictionaries, which are an extrinsic aid.

Although the literal rule keeps judges applying the law instead of creating it, it can also lead to some seemingly unfair outcomes as in *Berriman*.

> 🅔 The candidate uses a valid case as illustration but there is no development or explanation of the point made.

The other way of statutory interpretation mentioned in the question is the purposive approach, which is favoured by the European Court of Justice. The purposive approach consists of using extrinsic aids such as law reports and similar cases to fill in the gaps. This is a step further than the mischief rule as it leaves more to the judge's discretion.

> 🅔 A couple of valid points are made here but there is no real definition of either the purposive approach or the mischief rule, and again there is insufficient development and illustration.

> Overall, the candidate has demonstrated some knowledge of the appropriate material but it is expressed in a limited way. There are only narrow and partial definitions, there

is little in the way of illustration, and what is included is not sufficiently developed. There is little material relevant for AO2, with some isolated and limited comments but no real attempt to engage in a discussion or to address the question set. Furthermore, no reference is made to the source.

## Using the source for question 1

Source 1 is an adaptation of several pages of a leading textbook on the English legal system. It does not focus absolutely on statutory interpretation because it is used to discuss the relative roles of judges and Parliament in law making and the development of law. Nevertheless, there is some useful information in the source that can help in answering the question.

For AO1:
- Lines 38–42: some indication of why statutory interpretation is needed, which could be useful in an introductory paragraph of an answer.
- Lines 44–46: a statement that is highly relevant to this question, that the 'primary task' of the judges is to 'give effect to the meaning of the words used'.
- Lines 50–51: another example of when interpretation is needed.
- Lines 52–54: repetition of this basic point but also a reference to extrinsic aids.
- Line 60: an example of a case where the literal rule was applied but Lord Denning suggested using the mischief rule instead.

For AO2:
- Lines 2–3: the fact that few would deny the law-making function of the judiciary.
- Lines 17–23: reference to the supremacy of Parliament and the reasons for accepting judicial law making.
- Lines 34–37: reference to judicial views on what judges can do and what should be left to Parliament.
- Lines 55–59: discussion on courts being faced with factual situations for which the statute does not provide guidance.
- Lines 60–66: criticisms of Lord Denning's views on interpretation by Lord Simonds.

There is also some information in the other sources that could be used. Examples include:
- Source 4, lines 13–15: reference to the meaning of 'appropriation' in *Hale* and whether the meaning argued by the defendant was 'contrary to common sense'.
- Source 9, lines 17–19: reference to the wording of the statute on the meaning of 'effective entry'.
- Source 10, lines 14–16: reference to the literal meaning of 'building'.
- Source 11, lines 6–11: reference to going back to the words of the statute for the meaning of entering a building or any part of a building as a trespasser.

### Extra information you should give in your answer

While you can find some information in the source, particularly some useful comment for AO2, for a good answer you will need to use your knowledge of the basic rules of statutory interpretation. To do this you will need to:

- Define both the literal and purposive approaches — there is a partial definition only of the first in the source.
- Provide examples of cases that illustrate each approach, e.g. *Fisher* v *Bell* for the literal approach and *Royal College of Nursing* v *DHSS* for the purposive approach.
- Refer to either the language rules or the use of intrinsic aids and extrinsic aids and explain how these fit with the different approaches.
- Identify that the literal rule seeks the meaning primarily from the words used, whereas the purposive approach allows judges to go beyond the words themselves.
- Identify problems in seeking Parliament's intention in relation to either. For example, the literal rule can lead to absurdity or injustice that would probably not have been Parliament's intention, while the purposive approach can offend the separation of powers theory and mean that the judges take over Parliament's function by legislating.
- Reach a reasoned conclusion.

# Robbery

**Discuss the ways in which the case of *Hale* in Source 4 gives effect to the intention of Parliament in passing s.8 of the Theft Act 1968.** (15 marks)

■ ■ ■

## A-grade answer

In *Hale*, the defendant argued that he could not be guilty of the offence of robbery because the theft had been completed by the time any force was applied to the victim. Section 8 of the Theft Act 1968 states that a person is only guilty of robbery if he/she steals and uses force, before or at the time of the theft, in order to do so. It is quite clear that Parliament's intention when passing this section of the Act was to protect the public from robbers — those who use force in order to steal.

> 🖉 This is a good start, showing that the candidate has a full understanding of what is required in the offence of robbery. This information is given in Source 2.

Therefore, it goes against common sense to argue that the theft in this case ceased once the jewellery box was taken. The court in the case ruled that the theft was still taking place when the force was applied. This would seem to be a sensible result since it is doubtful that Parliament would have intended to allow robbers to escape conviction of the offence, merely because of a technical argument. The use of the hand over the mouth and the later tying up of the victim can easily be considered as force according to the case of *Dawson*. The taking of the jewellery box clearly amounts to a theft and so the defendant can be found guilty of robbery. However, if Parliament's intentions were interpreted using the literal rule then it would seem that the courts would, in fact, have added something different to Parliament's real intention. On the other hand, if the purposive approach is used then it could be argued that the court has simply extended the principle to a novel situation.

> 🖉 This appears to be a rather brief answer but, in fact, it contains a lot that the examiner wants to see. The candidate has indicated enough of the facts of the case to imply, if not expressly state, that the key issue in the case was the time at which the force was used in relation to the appropriation. Besides this, the candidate has clearly explained the requirements of the section. There is not quite enough material for maximum AO1 marks but certainly enough for Level 4. For AO2, the candidate has made four good points, albeit briefly stated: the basis of the argument by the defendant about when force was applied; the fact that it would be against common sense to accept this argument; the application of the continuing act principle; and some good comment on use of the different rules of interpretation. Although brief, the response shows excellent understanding of the issues for maximum AO2 marks. Overall, this constitutes a strong A-grade answer to the question.

# OCR Unit 2573

## C-grade answer

Parliament's intention in the offence of robbery is clearly stated in s.8(1) of the Theft Act 1968. The *actus reus* of robbery includes the elements of the *actus reus* of theft, which is the appropriation of property belonging to another. In addition, for the purposes of robbery there must be force present with the theft. The *mens rea* of robbery is the intention to put or seek to put an individual in fear of being then and there subjected to force (see Source 2). It also includes the necessary *mens rea* of theft — dishonesty and the intention of permanently depriving the other of the property.

> The candidate has identified some of the essential elements of robbery and included the elements of theft. However, this response would not gain all the marks that it could have done because the candidate has omitted one significant aspect of the offence, that the force is used in order to steal, and has merely stated that there must be 'force present with the theft'. Further, the candidate would not gain credit for a general reference to Source 2 in this way.

The case of *Hale* involves the issue of force being applied immediately before or during the theft. This is stated clearly for the purposes of robbery in the Theft Act 1968. This is Parliament's intention and Parliament would want this to be reflected in the cases being dealt with by judges.

> The candidate would gain credit for recognising the importance of the issue of when the force was applied in the case, but it could have been more clearly expressed, with some detailed explanation of how the point actually fits into the facts of the case.

However, Parliament's intention was only partially reflected in the case of *Hale*. This is because the continuing act theory was used by the judges. The continuing act theory has been developed through the common law and judges have applied it where force is involved for the purposes of robbery.

> Again, the candidate is making a good point but this could have been explained in more detail or developed further in order to secure higher marks.

In *Hale*, the force was applied to the victim after the appropriation had taken place. After the defendant stole the victim's property, he then applied force by proceeding to tie her up. Parliament's intention was that force should be applied before or during the appropriation, but it was allowed by the judge that the force could be applied after the appropriation if the jury could see that the appropriation was a continuing act. However, the continuing act must be within reasonable parameters.

> The candidate has a good understanding of the significance of the case but would lose out on gaining higher marks by not developing or explaining points fully. Despite all the references to the timing of the events, the examiner has to assume that the candidate understands that the important point is that the force is used in order to steal. For

# A2 Law

## question

AO1 the candidate otherwise shows good understanding of the elements of the offence, but has given only minimal detail on the significant factual elements of the case that create the problem for the judges to resolve. Two reasonable AO2 points are made: one in depth about what Parliament's intention was in s.8; the other, not fully explained, on the continuing act theory. Overall, the candidate has demonstrated adequate knowledge and made some good evaluative points for a typical C-grade answer.

■ ■ ■

## E-grade answer

Section 8 of the Theft Act 1968 states that robbery involves using force or creating fear while stealing something from the victim.

*e* The candidate has understood the importance of the definition of robbery, but has given a limited definition and missed the significant point that the force must be used 'in order to steal'.

In *R v Hale* (1978), the defendants tried to steal a jewellery box from the victim. Once they had got it they tied the victim up. The court held that as force was used, they were convicted of robbery because they were still in the process of stealing.

*e* Again, the candidate appreciates that the relative timing of the appropriation and the force are significant but does not express this in sufficient depth or detail, leaving it for the examiner to surmise the point that is being made.

The rules laid out in the Theft Act 1968 section 8 about robbery are quite different to *Hale* because force was used but not until after they had taken the jewellery box. Therefore, the statement in the Act was applied differently in this case, so Parliament's intention as to what counts as robbery is not very clear.

*e* The candidate shows some understanding of the problem in *Hale* relating to the time when force was applied but does not really develop or explain the point clearly.

Another case where force was used during the process of stealing is *R v Robinson*, where the defendant threatened the victim with a knife in order to get a payment he was owed and was convicted of robbery. Parliament's intentions are not always clear. The meanings are not always clear and are applied differently.

*e* There is not really anything of credit in this part of the answer.

Overall, this is a typical E-grade answer, as the material presented lacks development. The candidate has hinted at some of the appropriate facts of the case and also at the definition of robbery but has not covered either in any depth. The candidate has also shown limited understanding of the importance of the time at which the force was used in relation to the theft and that this does not fit absolutely with the definition in the section of the Act. Again, these points are not explained with clarity.

## Using the source for question 2

Source 4 is an adaptation of the judgement in the case of *Hale*, so for this question 2 there is extensive information that can help in answering the question. On other occasions, the case chosen for question 2 may only briefly be referred to in the source, possibly only by name. You should still be able to gain information from the source by looking at the context in which the case is mentioned.

For AO1:
- Lines 2–4: the basis of the offence of robbery — using force 'immediately before or at the time of stealing' and 'in order to steal'.
- Lines 2–5: some of the facts of the case, that there was some force used after the theft of a jewellery box.
- Line 24: this force involved tying the victim up after the jewellery box was seized.
- Line 29: the crime also involved putting a hand over the victim's mouth to stop her calling for help.

For AO2:
- Lines 4–6: reference to the defence that there could be no robbery because the force was used after the jewellery box was seized and so could not have been 'in order to steal'.
- Lines 6–9: the definition of theft.
- Lines 9–15: some discussion on the meaning of appropriation, including the judge's point that it would be 'contrary to common sense' to hold that the appropriation is over as soon as the defendant lays his hands on the property.
- Lines 19–26: the judge's explanation of the continuing act theory and how it applies to the facts of the case.
- Line 29: the judge's conclusion that the jury would be entitled to conclude that the act of tying the victim up was done in order to steal so that the defendant can be found guilty of robbery, having used force in order to steal.

There is also some useful information in the other sources. Examples include:
- Source 2 contains the definition of robbery from s.8 of the Theft Act 1968.
- Source 3 contains some discussion of the meaning of force that could be applied to the factual circumstances in the case. In lines 13–14 force is identified as an 'ordinary' word which 'juries understand'. In lines 14–19 it is explained that jostling a man must be done in a substantial way in order for it to be classed as force for the purposes of burglary.
- Source 6, lines 2–3 identify that 'very little may be required to turn a case of theft into one of robbery'. Lines 4–5 identify that a push causing a person to lose his/her balance could be sufficient force. Lines 15–17 identify that 'a struggle, even a fleeting one' can amount to sufficient force and uses the example of 'where an earring is snatched, tearing the lobe of the ear'.

### Extra information you should give in your answer

Most of the basic information that you will need in your answer can be found in the source. You also need to:
- Identify in your own words the key issue in the case, i.e. whether the defendants could be said to be using force immediately before or at the time of stealing.

**question**

- Recognise the important element of s.8, that the force is used in order to steal.
- Consider whether or not the judgement does give effect to Parliament's intention in the Act.
- Recognise the significance of the meaning given to appropriation and compare it with that in cases such as *Gomez* and *Atakpu*.

# Burglary (1)

In *Collins* (1973), Lord Justice Edmund Davies identified that a conviction for burglary is impossible unless it can be shown that a defendant made a 'substantial and effective entry' as a trespasser.

Discuss the extent to which developments in the case law concerning burglary mean that the above statement is an accurate description of the offence of burglary.

(25 marks)

■ ■ ■

## A-grade answer

One of the essential elements of the offence of burglary is that a person cannot be convicted of the offence unless he or she not only enters the premises but does so as a trespasser. This is clearly identified in the offence itself (see Source 7, lines 3 and 5).

> *e* This is an excellent start to the answer. The candidate has appreciated not only the point about the entry but also the significance of the trespass. It shows precise use of the source, with the lines where the trespass requirement is stated being clearly identified. Source 7 is the extract from s.9 of the Theft Act 1968. The first line identified by the candidate is the appropriate part of the s.9(1)(a) offence and the second line identified is the appropriate part of the s.9(1)(b) offence.

The Theft Act 1968 s.9(1)(a) deals with a burglary where the defendant enters a building or part of a building as a trespasser with the intention (*mens rea*) to commit theft, criminal damage or GBH, which was seen in the case of *Collins*.

> *e* The candidate shows good knowledge here of the essential elements of the offence charged in *Collins*.

In this case, the defendant had the intention of going into the house in order to rape the girl (an intention to rape was also covered by the offence at the time of the case). However, the girl had in fact consented to his entry by inviting him in when he was actually outside the window with his foot over the window sill, so the defendant could not be said to be trespassing. He also had sexual intercourse with the woman with her consent since she believed, in the dark, that it was her boyfriend who was paying her a nocturnal visit.

Therefore, there was no burglary without the trespass. The judge said that there could be no conviction for the offence unless the trespass occurred, and this would only be if the defendant had already made a substantial and effective entry into the building when the invitation for him to enter was made by the woman.

> *e* The candidate has focused in a succinct way on the critical factual elements of the case and on how these impact on the commission of the offence.

**question**

However, in s.9(1)(b) of the Theft Act 1968 it is stated that a burglary can also occur where the defendant enters a building or part of a building as a trespasser and then goes on either to steal or to commit GBH.

*e* The candidate shows good knowledge of the s.9(1)(b) offence.

The original statement made by Lord Justice Edmund Davies in the case of *Collins* is that there must be an effective and substantial entry by the defendant in order for the offence of burglary to take place.

However, this definition from *Collins* was widened in the case of *Brown* (Source 9). In this case, the Court of Appeal decided that the entry must indeed be 'effective' but it need not be 'substantial'. So an entry need not mean that the defendant's whole body is in the building, for example in *Brown*, where the top half of the defendant's body was leaning over inside the shop window but the bottom half of his body was outside the shop as he was stood on the pavement outside. This entry was effective because he was able to reach what he was trying to steal, but it was not actually substantial, and on this basis the Court of Appeal decided that it could still accept a conviction.

*e* This is a good use of the facts, and the candidate shows a clear understanding of how Lord Justice Edmund Davies's definition has been developed in the later case.

However, in the case of *Ryan* (Source 9) there was yet another development. The court applied the principle from *Brown* but this was complicated because of the facts of the case. This was because the defendant had got his head and neck trapped in the window and he could not possibly do anything further.

Realistically, this means that the entry was neither effective nor substantial. However, the court clearly focused on what the defendant's intention was at the time which was to commit one of the offences in s.9(2), so the defendant could be said to have committed burglary.

*e* Once again, there is good use of the facts. The candidate also highlights the important distinctions between the cases and underlines how this leads to yet another development.

The statement then is not entirely true, since the interpretation of an entry needing to be 'effective and substantial' has been considerably widened or developed so that the entry does not have to be either effective or substantial, as long as there is some form of entry.

This is not necessarily a good development because a person can receive up to 14 years in prison if convicted of burglary. This could happen even if the person gets stuck in the window and is then unable to do anything more. So it seems as though the interpretation is very prosecution friendly.

However, there are good points and people may consider it to be fair because the fact that the defendant intended to go on and commit a crime should be enough to make an entry like this a burglary.

> *e* The candidate has tried very hard in these last three paragraphs to make some evaluative comments about the developments and to reach some reasoned conclusions, thus demonstrating good essay-writing skills.
>
> There is clear evidence of preparation and planning in this answer and the candidate has tried to use all of the critical information to create an overall discussion with conclusions that attempt to answer the question set. There are parts that might have been more developed, but this is generally a good example of effective essay-writing technique and would be awarded a grade A.

■ ■ ■

## C-grade answer

This involves the character of the entry by the defendant for the purposes of burglary. In the case of *Collins*, Lord Justice Edmund Davies established that there must be an 'effective and substantial' entry by the defendant in order for the trespass to amount to a burglary.

The case decided that 'substantial' could be used to refer to any part of the body that was entering a building or part of a building (or any other structure identified in s.9(4) of the Theft Act 1968).

> *e* This is simplifying the situation but the candidate has the general idea.

'Effective' referred to the entry being effective for the purposes of stealing anything in a building or part of a building.

> *e* On the facts of *Collins*, strictly speaking, the candidate should have referred to the intention to rape rather than to steal. Nevertheless he/she sees the point that under s.9(1)(a) the defendant must enter as a trespasser with the intention of committing, at the time of the case, one of the four ulterior offences identified in s.9(2).

The facts of *Collins* are that the defendant, who was naked at the time, climbed up a ladder that he had leaned against the side of a house by a girl's window. The girl who was inside the room saw the defendant and then welcomed him into the room through the window. The girl, who was drunk, then allowed the man to have sex with her under the mistaken belief that he was in fact her boyfriend. She later realised that he was not her boyfriend half way through sexual intercourse and she slapped him on the face and told him to get out.

> *e* The facts in *Collins* are not absolutely accurate here but the candidate broadly outlines the case.

The point at which the defendant was actually invited into the room by the girl was an issue of great dispute in this case. If he had already entered through the window into the room and then had been invited inside by the girl then he would have been liable for burglary with the intention of raping her. However, if he had not actually entered the window and then was invited in he would not have been liable for burglary with intent to rape because there would have been no trespass.

> *e* The explanation here is somewhat woolly, but the candidate appreciates the importance of where Collins was at the time when the girl invited him in. He/she could have used the first paragraph of Source 8 where Lord Justice Edmund Davies's judgement clarifies the problem.

On appeal the defendant's conviction was quashed. This is because it was never put forward to the jury whether the defendant entered the premises as a trespasser or not.

> *e* Again, the candidate understands the point but could have explained it more clearly and developed it further.

In the case of *Brown*, the defendant was caught with half of his body in a shop window rummaging through some goods, or was trying to reach out for some goods. The defendant was convicted of burglary with the intent to steal. The court decided in this case that there did not have to be a substantial entry into the building as long as the entry was effective, so that he could be a trespasser without any substantial entry. This means that the definition has become prosecution friendly.

> *e* The candidate clearly understands the significance of the development in *Brown* but does not really explain why the entry was not substantial and why it was effective.

In the case of *Ryan*, the defendant was found with his head and arm stuck in a window. It was concluded in the case that the defendant had made an effective entry and so therefore it was an effective trespass.

> *e* Again, the candidate clearly understands that there is an important development in the case but does not really explain what it was. There is nothing here to tell the examiner why the conviction was upheld.

In *Ryan*, the effective entry test from *Brown* was confirmed and there only needs to be an effective entry not a substantial entry.

After the case of *Ryan* the courts are starting to become more prosecution friendly, as now it can be questioned whether there actually needs to be an effective entry at all. The law therefore has greatly developed since the case of *Collins*.

A trespass is an entry without consent into a building or a part of a building or a structure identified in s.9(4).

> *e* The final paragraph shows a lack of planning and is an extra piece of information that appears almost as an afterthought. The candidate has already reached a conclusion in the preceding paragraph. It would have been better exam technique to insert this paragraph at a more appropriate point in the essay rather than to add it here.
>
> Overall, the candidate knows that there are some important developments running through the three cases and is able to identify some of the critical issues. However,

the points are never fully explained and could have been developed further. There is an over-reliance on the facts of the individual cases, without the importance of the crucial facts being fully explained. The candidate also tries to reach a conclusion but this is limited in scope and only repeats what has already been said elsewhere in the essay, again with little in the way of detailed explanation or development. This is a reasonable essay showing adequate knowledge and identifying most of the obvious points, but it lacks the clarity and the development of comment that are necessary in order to secure an A or B grade. The candidate could have made better use of Source 9 where the important points of both *Brown* and *Ryan* are explained.

## E-grade answer

Section 9 of the Theft Act 1968 provides that a person can be convicted of a charge of burglary if he has trespassed into a building in order to steal something inside the building or to do some criminal damage inside the building, or to rape or to cause grievous bodily harm to someone who is inside the building,

 The candidate has provided a reasonable definition of the s.9(1)(a) offence, but does not specifically identify it as such and use it as a general definition of burglary. If there had been a little more attention to detail, the candidate could have achieved much higher marks.

The statement made in the case of *Collins* that there has to be an 'effective and substantial entry' in order for a person to be convicted of burglary has been shown not always to be the case in many situations. Sometimes people have been convicted for a burglary even when they have not made a full entry into a building that they have no permission to enter, which makes them a trespasser.

 Again, the candidate could have achieved higher marks by explaining why the requirement of 'effective and substantial entry' was given this definition in *Collins*.

In the case of *Ryan*, the defendant was found with his head and right arm trapped in the window of a building that he had had no permission to enter. The defendant was convicted of a burglary and so he appealed, arguing that he could not be convicted of burglary because he could not enter the building in the circumstances. However, his appeal failed because of the fact that part of him was inside the building and he did have the intention of trespassing and so this was enough for him to be convicted for burglary.

It could be questioned whether the defendant's entry was actually effective and substantial, as he was not completely in the building and he could not do anything because he was trapped. Therefore, it could be argued that trespassing always amounts to a burglary if the defendant is intending to commit one of the offences when he is inside, but the entry does not always have to be effective and substantial. *Ryan* develops *Collins*, making it much easier to prove that there is a burglary.

> ℮ The candidate makes some good AO2 points in these last two paragraphs, but they are not clearly expressed and could have been developed in order to gain higher marks.

In another case, *Smith and Jones*, the defendant was charged with burglary after he was found stealing a television set from his father's house. Although he obviously had permission to enter his father's house, the court held that it was still trespassing because he went beyond the permission given to him by his father and therefore he was charged with burglary. So again, this case demonstrates that no effective or substantial entry needs to be made in order to be convicted for burglary.

> ℮ It is arguable how appropriate this case is here. The candidate does not properly explain why it is being used or its relevance to the question that is being asked.

It could be that these words are interpreted by Parliament in a different way to what we would define them as and this is why the courts are making the decisions that they make.

> ℮ It is difficult to understand exactly what the candidate means here, so little credit could be given.

Overall, the candidate has shown some understanding of what the issues are and has used one of the relevant cases in *Ryan*. However, too much is left undeveloped. The candidate has failed to mention the case of *Brown*, which logically should have been considered before *Ryan*. This is an example of a candidate missing what is available in the source materials, since Source 9 covers both cases. The candidate could also have used the case of *Collins* more in order to explain the significance of the requirement. This is a patchy answer and typical of grade E, being short on detailed knowledge and not displaying the best exam skills.

## Using the sources for question 3

Source 8 is a sizeable extract adapted from the judgement in *Collins*, so there is a great deal of information here that may be useful in answering the question. In addition, Source 9 contains information on the cases of *Brown* and *Ryan* that discussed or developed the principle on 'effective and substantial entry'. This is a good example of how being knowledgeable about what is in the sources beforehand can be of benefit to you in the exam itself. When you consider the overarching theme of the development of law it is always worth looking at the sources immediately before and after the one in question, as there is a good chance that they will show some development. Material that is helpful here includes:

### Source 8
For AO1:
- Lines 1–5: some brief facts from the case.
- Lines 6–10: the key elements of the offence.
- Lines 13–26: three different interpretations of the meaning of 'trespass'.
- Lines 27–31: the interpretation of 'trespass' preferred by the court in the case.

For AO2:
- Lines 38–41: the meaning of 'entry' given by the court in the case.

*Source 9*
For AO1:
- Lines 4–5: the basic facts of *Brown*.
- Lines 5–6: the basic facts of *Ryan*.

For AO2:
- Line 1: the fact that the judgement in Brown widened the meaning given to 'entry' in *Collins*.
- Lines 3–4: the fact that the whole of the body does not have to be in the building for an effective entry.
- Lines 6–7: the fact that the Court of Appeal in *Ryan* applied the principle in Brown.
- Lines 11–13: the fact that 'effective' does not have to mean 'effective to commit the ulterior offence' and also some justification for this principle.
- Lines 17–19: further support for this principle.
- Lines 20–21: the view that the two cases may be leading to a point where the entry need be neither substantial nor effective for a conviction.

There is also some useful information in some other sources:
- Source 7 contains the definitions of burglary in s.9 of the Theft Act 1968.
- Source 12 (lines 1–6) contains a discussion on the definition of the word 'trespass'.

## Extra information you should give in your answer

A lot of useful information for your answer can be found in the sources. However, you also need to discuss:
- the fact that the definition of entry is purely case led and is not defined in the Act
- the fact that even in *Collins* it was accepted that the whole body does not need to be in the building for the offence to occur
- why Lord Justice Edmund Davies felt the need to define the term 'entry' in *Collins*
- how small a part of the body entering the building is necessary for a conviction
- whether or not there is a development in the principle
- whether this development is for policy reasons
- why the judges declared the law as they did in *Brown* and *Ryan*

# Burglary (II)

Using the definition of burglary in section 9 of the Theft Act 1968 and appropriate case law in support, consider whether a conviction for burglary is possible in each of the following three situations:

(a) Alphonse enters Bopinder's newsagent's one evening, intending to steal the takings. In fact, when Alphonse enters he discovers that Bopinder has already taken that day's takings and deposited the money in the night safe at the bank. Alphonse becomes angry because there is no money to steal and so he breaks both of Bopinder's arms. (10 marks)

(b) Carys invites Damian to have a drink with her in the motorhome in which she lives. While Carys is getting the drinks Damian looks through the open bedroom door and spots Carys's expensive watch lying on the bed. He quickly goes into the bedroom and steals the watch. (10 marks)

(c) Elise falls out with her best friend Françoise when she discovers that Françoise has been going out with her (Elise's) boyfriend behind her back. Elise breaks into Françoise's flat intending to beat her up and cause her serious harm but finds that Françoise is not at home. Elise becomes even angrier because Françoise is not there and so she cuts up all of Françoise's clothes with scissors, destroying them all. (10 marks)

**Total: 30 marks**

■ ■ ■

## A-grade answer

(a) Section 9(1)(a) of the Theft Act 1968 states that a defendant is guilty of burglary if he/she enters a building or part of a building with the intention of stealing anything therein (Source 7, lines to 2–4 and line 8).

> 🖉 This is a good start to the answer. The candidate has seen that the facts indicate a possible s.9(1)(a) offence, has provided the appropriate definition of the offence and has used the appropriate source effectively.

Alphonse enters the newsagent's with the intention of stealing money. The fact that there is no money for him to steal when he enters does not matter according to the case of *R v Walkington* (conditional intent is sufficient). However, the question arises here whether he enters the building in fact as a trespasser, when it is most likely that as a potential customer he has consent to enter. This does not matter as a result of the case of *Jones and Smith*, as Alphonse enters in such a way that goes beyond the consent that would be given by Bopinder, since he enters with the intention of stealing.

> 🖉 This shows excellent understanding of the offence, and appropriate cases are used effectively in applying the law.

OCR Unit 2573

The fact that Alphonse has entered the newsagent's shop and that he has then beaten up Bopinder, breaking both of his arms, means that he commits burglary under s.9(1)(b), which states that he is guilty if, having entered, he then goes on to commit GBH.

> *e* The candidate has spotted the s.9(1)(b) offence, defined the law and applied it appropriately to the facts in the problem.

Alphonse has entered a building (the shop), he has entered as a trespasser intending to steal from it, and he has inflicted GBH on Bopinder. Alphonse is guilty under both s.9(1)(a) and s.9(1)(b) of the Theft Act 1968.

> *e* This is a full answer, applying all of the law appropriately and easily gains the maximum 10 marks for this part of the question.

**(b)** Section 9(1)(b) of the Theft Act 1968 states that a defendant is guilty of burglary if he/she has entered a building or part of a building as a trespasser and either steals or attempts to steal (Source 7, lines 5–7).

> *e* Again, the candidate has seen the significance of the facts and has provided a definition of the s.9(1)(b) offence, making good use of the source to reinforce it.

Damian has been invited into Carys's motorhome. According to s.9 of the Theft Act 1968 a building can also include an inhabited vehicle. The motor home is a vehicle, and Carys lives in it, and so it is an inhabited vehicle.

> *e* The candidate, surprisingly in view of what has been written so far, has not cited s.9(4) here which would have given complete detail to the answer.

The fact that Carys has invited Damian into the motorhome for a drink means that he has consent to be there. However, in the case of *Jones and Smith* the court stated that a person could then be a trespasser if he exceeds the terms of the consent given. It is reasonable to assume that Carys would not have given Damian consent to enter in order to steal her watch. Furthermore, it could be argued that Damian has entered a restricted area by going into Carys's bedroom, and that this can be viewed as a part of a building as in *R v Walkington*.

> *e* The candidate has made good use of both *Jones and Smith* and *Walkington* here to demonstrate that Damian is in fact trespassing for the purposes of a burglary charge.

Therefore, Damian could be classed as a trespasser. He stole the watch when he saw it. He is therefore guilty of burglary under s.9(1)(b), as he has entered a building or part of a building as a trespasser and has gone on to steal the watch.

> *e* This is another very good answer. Only the actual citation of s.9(4) and some reference to a possible s.9(1)(a) offence could have improved it.

**(c)** Elise has broken into Françoise's flat and she has therefore entered as a trespasser, as Françoise has not given her any consent to enter in this way, despite the fact

# A2 Law

that they are friends. It is also an effective and substantial entry according to *Collins*. Elise had the intent before entering the flat as a trespasser to beat Françoise up and cause her serious harm, which means that she entered intending to inflict GBH. Clearly, the flat will also count as a building (Source 10, lines 14–15).

> *e* The last sentence shows that the candidate is acquainted with all the source materials because Source 10 is specifically about the definitions of building provided in various cases.

Therefore, Elise has entered the building as a trespasser with the intent to inflict GBH and is guilty under s.9(1)(a) of the Theft Act 1968.

> *e* So far the candidate has given a very good answer on the possible s.9(1)(a) offence.

Furthermore, the fact that she enters the flat and then destroys all of Françoise's clothes constitutes the offence of criminal damage, which is another offence of which she can be found guilty under s.9(1)(a). The fact that she did not have the intent to commit this offence beforehand does not matter as she had the conditional intent to commit some offence (*Walkington*).

> *e* The candidate answers in error on this last point and has not spotted that there could be no s.9(1)(a) offence for the criminal damage, as Elise did not enter intending to commit it. He/she has also overlooked the fact that s.9(1)(b) does not include criminal damage, so that is unavailable.

Overall, the candidate would be awarded virtually maximum marks for parts (a) and (b). However, while part of (c) is well answered there is one significant aspect of the facts that is not dealt with appropriately. Nevertheless, there is sufficient here for a grade A. The candidate displays good exam technique, both in the use of detailed law and the references to the sources in support.

■ ■ ■

## C-grade answer

(a) For an offence of burglary to be committed under s.9(1)(a) of the Theft Act 1968 there has to be an entry as a trespasser with the intention of committing one of the offences mentioned in s.9(2) of the Act.

> *e* This is a good start. The candidate spots the possibility of a s.9(1)(a) offence and defines it, although he/she could have gone further by identifying the ulterior offences.

Although Alphonse did not actually break into the shop, he still entered as a trespasser because he went into the shop intending to steal the takings and theft is one of the offences mentioned in s.9(2). This can still be a trespass, even though the newsagent's shop is a public place, and Alphonse would not normally be considered to be a trespasser by entering it, as the public would generally have the consent of the owner to enter. In addition, the shop owner, Bopinder, clearly would never have given Alphonse permission to enter the shop if he knew that Alphonse was going to steal from him, as in *Jones and Smith*.

> 🅔 The candidate has made a reasoned case for why Alphonse can be classed as a trespasser, using appropriate case law, and has also identified the appropriate ulterior offence.

The fact that Alphonse entered intending to steal but instead went on to commit an offence of GBH, probably under s.20 of the Offences Against the Person Act 1861, makes no difference. Both of these offences, theft and GBH, are mentioned in s.9(2) and so even though Alphonse did not commit the offence of theft, he still went into the newsagent's intending to steal and so he should still be liable for burglary.

> 🅔 The candidate has given a very good answer to one part of the question but has not dealt with the GBH and the possible s.9(1)(b) offence. Had he/she done so, the response would have gained maximum marks.

**(b)** Section 9(1) of the Theft Act 1968 states that a person can be found guilty of burglary if he/she enters a building or a part of a building as a trespasser with the intention of committing any offence contained in s.9(2).

> 🅔 This is a reasonable start and a good definition, but the candidate has omitted the '(a)' from the offence.

All of these issues can be debated. First, there is the issue of whether a motorhome can constitute a building for the purposes of burglary. Section 9(4) of the Act states that a building can also be a vehicle that is inhabited. So, for the purposes of burglary, a motorhome like Carys's can be classed as a building because she lives in it.

> 🅔 Although it could have been stated more succinctly and the candidate could have used what is actually said in the subsection, this response still shows good understanding.

There is also the issue of whether Damian entered the building as a trespasser, as Carys invited him into the motorhome. However, the consent she gave him only extended as far as going in for a drink, which did not involve him going into the bedroom. As in *Jones and Smith*, the consent was not given to enter the building in order to commit a theft. The part of the building that Damian entered is an issue too. This is the same point as in *Walkington*. Damian was not a trespasser at the time he went into the motorhome, but he did become one when he saw the watch in the bedroom and went in there (part of a building) with the intent to steal it. So, in that sense, Damian has committed burglary and he should be convicted.

> 🅔 Overall, the candidate uses law well, although there could have been some more detail in parts of the answer. One omission that otherwise could have secured higher marks is the possible s.9(1)(b) offence.

**(c)** Looking at the definition of building in s.9 of the Theft Act 1968, the Act does cover flats as buildings. Because of this, when Elise broke into Françoise's flat she was entering a building. She was also entering the flat as a trespasser because she broke in and had no right to be there. She entered intending to beat up Françoise and cause her serious harm. From this it can be assumed that she was not just going to commit an assault or an ABH but it was going to be GBH. Again, it does not matter that she committed the offence of criminal damage rather than GBH because she *intended* to commit GBH. The Criminal Damage Act states that there needs to be either intent by the defendant or recklessness as to destroying or damaging property belonging to another. All these are actually satisfied by Elise and so she did enter a building with the intent to commit an offence. However, it would not have mattered if she did not commit any offence; the fact that she entered with the intent is sufficient. So on the facts here Elise is guilty and should be convicted of burglary under s.9.

> Some good points are made here, but the candidate does not actually identify under which section Elise should be charged. The trespass issue could have been developed further. The candidate shows understanding of the fact that for s.9(1)(a) the ulterior offence does not have to be carried out, intent is sufficient, but does not express this very clearly. The problem associated with the criminal damage making a s.9(1)(b) offence impossible is not considered either. The candidate would only be awarded a few token marks for this part for some appropriate reasoning.
>
> Overall, the candidate makes good use of law and there is some good application in parts (a) and (b), although some areas could have been more developed. Part (c), however, is much weaker. Taken as a whole, the answer shows adequate knowledge and most of the appropriate law has been applied to achieve a grade C.

■ ■ ■

### E-grade answer

**(a)** This depends on whether the shop was closed when Alphonse went into it intending to steal the takings. This is because if Alphonse did go into the shop when it was closed to the public then he would have entered as a trespasser with the intention of stealing from the shop, and he then went on to inflict GBH on Bopinder. Therefore he is a burglar and can be convicted. However, if the shop was still open when Alphonse went into it, then he did not enter as a trespasser but as a member of the public — he cannot be convicted of a burglary because he would have Bopinder's consent to enter the shop. However, he could be convicted of robbery instead because with robbery you do not have to get away with anything in order to be convicted, as long as you use force. If Alphonse entered as a trespasser with the intention of stealing then he could be convicted of burglary because he committed GBH on Bopinder.

> 🖊 The candidate wrestles with the problem of proving the trespass, applying some common-sense reasoning rather than the appropriate law. The candidate would gain some credit for the first part of the last sentence, which is limited explanation but correct, although the reasoning then goes astray in the final part of the sentence.

**(b)** Damian cannot be seen as a trespasser under the Theft Act 1968 because Carys invited him to go there. Therefore, he has not entered as a trespasser. However, Carys did not invite him to go into her bedroom, so when he entered her bedroom he became a trespasser. Also, when he looked into her bedroom and saw the watch he decided to steal it, and so when he did enter her bedroom he entered as a trespasser with the intention of committing a theft of the watch.

> 🖊 The candidate is making the point from *Walkington* here and would gain some credit, but the point is not developed and could have been made more effectively using the appropriate citation.

Damian did take Carys's watch and this is sufficient for theft and so he is guilty of burglary when he goes in and takes the watch.

> 🖊 Again, this is possibly a reference to the s.9(1)(b) offence but insufficient detail is given, although some limited credit would be given for correct reasoning.

It can also be classed as burglary because Carys lives in the motorhome and so it can be classed as inhabited and this means it is a building under the Theft Act. This means that Damian should be convicted of burglary.

> 🖊 The candidate has appreciated the significance of the fact that Carys lives in a motorhome. Some limited reasoning is given, for which limited credit would be given, but higher marks could have been achieved by using full citation. The candidate has shown some understanding in part (b) but the reasoning is based more on common sense than on applying appropriate law.

**(c)** Elise has, in fact, entered Françoise's flat as a trespasser and it does not matter that she is her friend and would normally be invited to go there because she has broken in this time and that is a trespass. However, it could be said that she did not have any intention of committing the unlawful damage when she entered the flat. It is not clear whether Elise actually intended to commit GBH because it only says that she intended to beat Françoise up and cause her serious damage and this does not have to mean GBH rather than just an assault. This would be for the jury to decide. If Elise did not enter the flat with the intention of committing GBH, then she cannot be convicted of burglary. What she will be convicted of is criminal damage under the Criminal Damage Act because she cut up all of Françoise's clothes, and this counts as damage or destruction under the Act and she can also be charged with breaking and entering. However, if Elise did enter the flat with the intention of inflicting GBH then it is possible that she could be convicted of burglary because she has entered the flat intending to commit GBH but has gone on and inflicted unlawful damage instead, which is enough for burglary.

*e* Again, the candidate struggles to apply common-sense reasoning rather than applying the law. Credit could be given for the last sentence, even though the last part of it strays away from correct reasoning. Some limited credit could be gained for the references to the trespass.

Overall, although the candidate has spotted some of the significant issues in the three scenarios and would gain credit for some of the reasoning, much of it is based on common sense rather than application of the law.

## Using the sources for question 4

The fact that question 4 is problem based and does not refer to a specific source should not prevent you from using the sources to help you with your answer. If you know the sources well before you go into the exam you will be able to refer directly to those parts that will help you. Question 4 will either involve problem questions on robbery or burglary, or some on each, so obvious examples of this are Source 2 and Source 7, which are extracts from s.8 and s.9 of the Theft Act 1968. These sections give you the essential elements of robbery and burglary respectively.

For robbery:
- Source 2 provides the basic definition of robbery from s.8 of the Theft Act 1968.
- Source 3, particularly lines 9–16, discusses the meaning of force from *Dawson*.
- Source 4 deals with the problem of the force being applied 'immediately before or at the time of stealing' and 'in order to steal' in *Hale*, and lines 12–15 show how the judge dealt with the issue.
- Source 5 again deals with the amount of force identified as necessary for robbery in *Corcoran* v *Anderton*, particularly in lines 12–19.
- Source 6 deals with the same issue in *Clouden*, particularly in lines 5–15.

For burglary:
- Source 7 provides the basic definition for both types of burglary and the extended definition of building from s.9 of the Theft Act 1968.
- Source 8 deals in detail with the issue of the trespass, particularly in lines 27–31, and the need for an 'effective and substantial entry' from *Collins*, particularly in lines 38–41.
- Source 9 covers the developments of the meaning of 'entry as a trespasser' in the cases of *Brown* and *Ryan*, with lines 10–13 and 17–19 being particularly important.
- Source 10 provides a range of support from case law on the meaning of 'building' with lines 3–5, 10–12 and 14–16 being particularly useful.
- Source 11 provides the meaning of 'part of a building' from *Walkington*, and also the issue of conditional intent.
- Source 12 deals with the issue of going beyond the terms of consent to enter a building in *Jones and Smith*, with lines 11–13 being particularly useful.

### Extra information you should give in your answer

The sources provide you with some of the essential law needed for answering the problem questions, but you will need to bring to this your own skills of applying the law accurately and in a reasoned way.

For part (a) you need to be able to:
- identify the circumstances in which a person enters a building as a trespasser, which is normally open to the public or for which they would normally have consent to enter
- distinguish between the s.9(1)(a) and the s.9(1)(b) offences
- know the ulterior offences for s.9(1)(a) and the linked offences for s.9(1)(b)
- understand the principle of conditional intent

For part (b) you need to be able to:
- understand the extended meaning of building in s.9(4)
- identify the meaning of 'part of a building' and the circumstances in which entering a building legitimately but then entering part of the building as a trespasser can occur
- distinguish between the s.9(1)(a) and the s.9(1)(b) offences

For part (c) you need to be able to:
- distinguish between the s.9(1)(a) and the s.9(1)(b) offences
- know the ulterior offences for s.9(1)(a) and the linked offences for s.9(1)(b)
- understand the principle of conditional intent